A TRUE BOOK

The Krakatau Eruption

PETER BENOIT

Children's Press®
An Imprint of Scholastic Inc.
New York Toronto London Auckland Sydney
Mexico City New Delhi Hong Kong
Danbury, Connecticut

Content Consultant
Richard S. Fiske, PhD
Geologist Emeritus
Smithsonian Institution
Washington, DC

Library of Congress Cataloging-in-Publication Data

Benoit, Peter, 1955–
  The Krakatau eruption/Peter Benoit.
      p. cm.—(A true book)
  Includes bibliographical references and index.
  ISBN-13: 978-0-531-20628-7 (lib. bdg.)   ISBN-13: 978-0-531-28997-6 (pbk.)
  ISBN-10: 0-531-20628-9 (lib. bdg.)   ISBN-10: 0-531-28997-4 (pbk.)
  1. Krakatoa (Indonesia)—Eruption, 1883—Juvenile literature. 2. Volcanoes—Indonesia—
Krakatoa—History—19th century—Juvenile literature. I. Title.
  QE523.K73B46 2011
  551.2109598'18—dc22   2010045930

All rights reserved. Published in 2011 by Children's Press, an imprint of Scholastic Inc.
Printed in the United States of America. 113
SCHOLASTIC, CHILDREN'S PRESS, A TRUE BOOK and associated logos are trademarks and/or registered trademarks of Scholastic Inc.

 3 4 5 6 7 8 9 10 R 18 17 16 15 14 13

Find the Truth!

Everything you are about to read is true *except* for one of the sentences on this page.

Which one is **TRUE**?

T or F Krakatau looks almost the same as it did in 1883.

T or F The eruptions on Krakatau affected weather around the world.

Find the answers in this book.

3

Contents

THE **BIG** TRUTH!

**Volcanic activity
on Krakatau**

Back in Action

Volcanic rocks are ground up for use in toothpaste and soap.

4 Other Effects of the Eruptions

5 Keeping an Eye on Krakatau

Krakatau before the August 27, 1883, explosion

The 1883 Krakatau eruption could be seen and heard thousands of miles away.

At the time of the eruption, Indonesia was known as the Dutch East Indies.

CHAPTER 1

An Amazing Explosion

On August 27, 1883, residents of Perth, Australia, awoke to a loud explosion. Meanwhile, workers on the island of Rodrigues in the Indian Ocean swore they heard cannon fire. What was causing these mysterious and frightening sounds? Thousands of miles away in Indonesia, volcanic activity was blasting apart an island called Krakatau (krak-uh-TOU). The volcanic **eruptions** there caused one of the most violent explosions in world history!

An Area of Volcanic Action

Indonesia has more **active volcanoes** than any other country on Earth. Many of them make up a curved chain of islands known as the Indonesian volcanic arc. Krakatau is one of these islands and is located in the Sunda Strait. This narrow stretch of water flows between two of the largest Indonesian islands—Java and Sumatra. The Sunda Strait joins the Java Sea to the Indian Ocean.

In fall 2010, Mount Merapi, located on the island of Java, experienced several powerful eruptions.

About 130 volcanoes in Indonesia have erupted in the past and could erupt again.

What Exactly Is a Volcano?

A volcano is a **vent**, or opening in Earth's **crust**. Gases and a hot liquid rock called **magma** flow through the vent. **Lava** is magma that reaches Earth's surface.

Pressure within a volcano is what causes it to erupt. An eruption forces out lava, dust, ash, gas, and pieces of rock. Some eruptions have the power to blast apart an entire island. This is what happened on Krakatau.

Most volcanic eruptions are small compared to the Krakatau eruption.

This map shows the location of Krakatau and the volcanic arc that runs the length of Indonesia.

Krakatau was called Fire Mountain during ancient times.

Earlier Eruptions on the Island

Krakatau and the nearby islands of Lang and Verlaten were once joined together. **Geologists** believe that they are the remains of a larger volcanic island. This ancient island was probably torn apart by an eruption in 416 C.E. Some experts also think that several other major eruptions might have occurred on Krakatau between then and 1680.

Proof From the Past

How do modern geologists know about volcanic activity that took place so long ago? Documents such as letters and journals describe what people heard and saw on Krakatau as far back as 416 C.E. These writings mention "thundering sounds" and "great glowing fires." But nothing prepared anyone for the eruption that shook Krakatau and much of the nearby world in 1883.

Even small volcanic eruptions are violent events.

There were smaller eruptions on Krakatau in the weeks leading up to August 27.

CHAPTER 2

Events Leading Up to August 1883

Were there any hints before August 27, 1883, that an eruption on Krakatau would be so violent? It is hard to tell. Modern geologists have carefully studied the months leading up to that date for clues. They do know a few facts. One is that the summer of 1883 was filled with earthquakes and a growing rumble from the mighty island volcano.

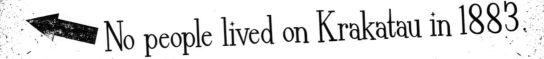 No people lived on Krakatau in 1883.

Krakatau's Cones

Before 1883, three main volcanic **cones** made up Krakatau. A cone is the mountain that forms around a vent. Rakata (rah-KAH-tah) was the tallest cone, at 2,667 feet (813 meters) above sea level. Danan (dah-nahn) rose 1,460 feet (445 m). Perboewatan (pair-bo-way-WAH-tahn) was the lowest and measured about 400 feet (122 m).

Rakata was chopped nearly in half by the power of the eruption.

Rakata was the only remaining cone after the eruption of 1883. The others were completely destroyed.

Earthquakes were a warning that something was happening beneath the surface of Krakatau.

An Abrupt End to the Quiet

It had been more than 200 years since Krakatau had erupted. Things were mostly quiet there until May 1883. Then three months of intense earthquakes began to shake the island. By May 20, a series of eruptions occurred in Perboewatan's vent. Ash and dust were blown 17 miles (27 kilometers) into the air. Residents of the Indonesian city of Jakarta—located about 100 miles (160 km) away—could hear the thunder of the eruptions.

Pumice floated so thickly on the Indian Ocean it supported the weight of sailors.

Most pumice is the size of small stones.

More Forceful Eruptions

The situation on Krakatau grew more unstable as the weeks passed. Soon, new vents opened around Danan. People witnessed thick, black clouds of smoke and ash hanging over the island for days at a time. **Pumice**, a lightweight volcanic rock, fell from the ash and smoke above. Eventually, pumice would be spotted floating more than 3,700 miles (6,000 km) away in the Indian Ocean.

A Growing Threat

Meanwhile, the earthquakes and volcanic activity created dangerous waves in the Sunda Strait. Some ships that were already held by anchors were also chained down to stop them from floating off! By late August, it was clear that the volcano would threaten areas hundreds of miles away.

The waters surrounding Krakatau were very dangerous during the summer of 1883.

August 26

On August 26, eruptions were occurring every 10 minutes on Krakatau. At 12:53 p.m., people on islands throughout the Sunda Strait reported hearing the loud roar of a violent volcanic explosion. Thick streams of ash and dust reached 17 miles (27 km) into the air. Hot pumice started raining down on the decks of ships 12 miles (19 km) away from the island.

Twelve volcanic eruptions had occurred by early August.

While many eruptions occurred on August 26, the most powerful ones were yet to come.

People had never experienced a volcanic eruption as massive as Krakatau.

The End of the World?

The eruptions continued creating ocean waves, which grew taller and more powerful. The rough water, smoky clouds, and trembling earth probably made it seem like the world was coming to an end. People who lived on nearby Indonesian islands or who were aboard ships in the Sunda Strait were filled with terror. They could not help but wonder what horrors the next day would bring.

The tsunamis caused by Krakatau were as deadly as the eruptions.

CHAPTER 3

A Day of Destruction

On August 27, 1883, the volcanic activity on Krakatau reached new levels of destruction. Four huge explosions created giant waves, or **tsunamis**, that rose 120 feet (37 m) high. These deadly walls of water washed over hundreds of Indonesian villages. The tsunamis, together with hot clouds of ash, gas, dust, and rock killed tens of thousands of people.

Tsunamis occurred as far away as San Francisco and the English Channel.

Water quickly turns into steam when it meets the heat of volcanic lava.

Deadly Darkness

The four major volcanic explosions that tore apart Krakatau on August 27 occurred at 5:30 a.m., 6:44 a.m., 8:20 a.m., and 10:02 a.m. During this time, the walls of the volcano started to collapse. Seawater poured over its crumbling sides and mixed with hot magma to create explosive steam.

The Biggest Blast

The last of the four explosions was the strongest. It is still considered one of the most violent explosions in world history. People 3,000 miles (5,000 km) away from Krakatau reported hearing and feeling the force of the blast. A blanket of ash and smoke hung 50 miles (80 km) above the ground. It cloaked an area of 300,000 square miles (800,000 sq km) in sudden darkness.

The Krakatau eruption was one of the first news items to spread quickly around the world by telegraph.

The Krakatau eruption was big news around the world.

23

Washed Away by Waves

Meanwhile, glowing clouds of hot volcanic gas, ash, dust, and rock swept outward from Krakatau. They flattened and burned everything in their path. The clouds quickly reached the shore of nearby Sumatra. The volcanic material traveled across the ocean waves on a thick bed of steam. This activity in the water and the force of the explosion created terrible tsunamis. Deadly waves washed over several low-lying islands in the Sunda Strait.

Tsunamis destroy everything in their paths.

Tsunamis destroyed 295 towns and villages on August 27.

The combination of lava, ash, gas, and tsunamis caused catastrophic death and destruction.

Lives Lost

Authorities later said that the tsunamis drowned more than 30,000 people. Burning volcanic gas, ash, dust, and rock caused another 4,500 deaths. Bodies continued to be found floating in the Indian Ocean well into September 1883. Most modern experts believe that the eruptions on August 27 killed a total of 36,417 men, women, and children.

About two-thirds of Krakatau disappeared on August 27.

Krakatau today is significantly smaller than before the 1883 eruption.

Once the Skies Cleared

The skies above Krakatau were as dark as night following the volcanic explosions on August 27. The damage to the island became obvious after the cloud of gas, ash, and dust finally cleared. Land that had once risen 400 to 1,400 feet (120 to 425 m) above sea level was suddenly no more than a deep pit in the ocean floor.

Suffering in the Sunda Strait

The destruction to Java and Sumatra was shocking. Railways were twisted like ribbons. The remains of houses and farms lay burned and broken into pieces.

The explosions on Krakatau tore apart countless communities. Several towns and villages in the Sunda Strait were never rebuilt. As time passed, though, people all over the world discovered that the eruptions caused more than death and damage to the landscape.

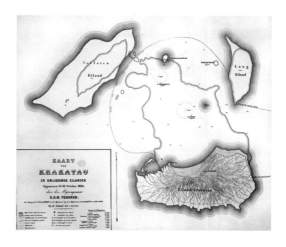

This map details the parts of Krakatau that remained above the water after the eruption.

Back in Action

After the 1883 eruption, Krakatau was quiet for many years. But on June 29, 1927, the crew of a fishing boat witnessed the mighty volcano's return. The men heard rumbling sounds coming from underwater as they hauled up their nets. Soon, large gas bubbles burst up and exploded. Krakatau had erupted for the first time in more than 40 years. Since then, it has continued to erupt from time to time.

By the early 1930s, Krakatau had released enough lava from the ocean floor to create a new island known as Anak Krakatau.

Small eruptions such as this one in 1995 continued to release more lava, ash, and gas.

Anak Krakatau has since grown to about 1,000 feet (300 m) tall. Small eruptions help the island continue to grow.

Like Krakatau, the eruption of Mount St. Helens in 1980 lowered temperatures around the world.

CHAPTER 4

Other Effects of the Eruptions

The extent of the damage caused by the volcanic eruptions was clear to anyone who visited Indonesia. But the explosions also led to changes in **climate** and **geography**. What happened on Krakatau that day affected everything from the color of sunsets to weather around the world.

 After it erupted, Mount St. Helens was 1,314 feet (401 m) shorter.

Wind carried volcanic ash from Krakatau all the way around the world. ➡️

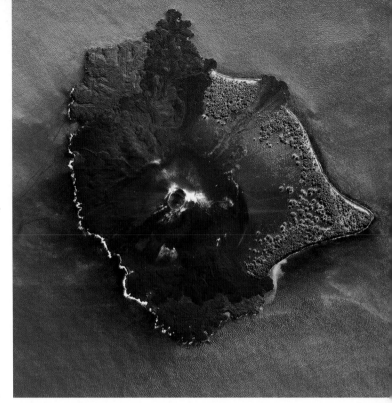

The new land features that built up after Krakatau's eruption have since worn away.

Sudden Changes

The volcanic ash, dust, and rock that fell from glowing clouds on August 27 settled into a thick layer on the ocean floor in the Sunda Strait. They also formed sandbars and briefly built up the size of islands such as Lang and Verlaten. Wind and water have worn away many of these new land features over time.

Scenic Sunrises and Sunsets

The eruptions created lovely sunrises and sunsets that were seen as far away as Europe and North America. This is because the explosions blew volcanic dust into Earth's **atmosphere**. It remained there for several months. Sunlight passing through the dust added amazing red, pink, orange, and purple colors to the sky. Writers and artists used poems and paintings to describe what they saw at sunrise and sunset.

Beautiful sunsets were one of the few good things caused by Krakatau's violent eruption.

33

A Cooler Climate

The eruptions on Krakatau affected climate patterns all over the world. Large amounts of ash and gas had been released into the atmosphere. This caused clouds to reflect more light than normal. This cooled the Earth more than usual. Average temperatures in the year following the explosions dropped by as much as 2.2 degrees Fahrenheit (1.2 degrees Celsius).

In 2010, Iceland's Eyjafjallajökul volcano released so much ash into the air that airplanes traveling to Europe were grounded for days.

Volcanologists are geologists who study volcanoes.

Volcanologists sometimes wear special suits to protect themselves from a volcano's heat.

What Scientists Have Learned

Scientists studied the effects of the 1883 eruptions on climate and geography with great interest. They also began trying to understand what led up to one of the most violent explosions in history. New technology has helped geologists learn a lot in the years since the eruptions occurred. Yet they still have many questions about the past, present, and future of Krakatau.

Today, Krakatau is a popular tourist destination.

CHAPTER 5

Keeping an Eye on Krakatau

Modern geologists have different ideas about what caused the violent eruptions on Krakatau. Volcanic activity has continued to occur in that part of the world. But nothing—not even the devastating eruptions of Indonesia's Mount Merapi in 2010— has matched the events of 1883. People around the world are both curious and fearful about whether anything will match them in the future.

What remains of Krakatau is now part of an Indonesian national park.

The pressure of steam within a volcano builds quickly if there is no way for it to be released.

A Steamy Situation

Some scientists believe the eruptions were so explosive because Krakatau's walls were collapsing. Ocean water flooded over the volcano's crumbling sides. This seawater then flowed into the hot magma and formed a lot of of steam. The pressure of the steam inside Krakatau could have made the explosions more powerful.

Magma Mix

Other geologists think hot magma may have suddenly mixed with cooler magma on August 27. This might have caused a pressure buildup inside the volcano that ended in a violent explosion. Scientists hope that discussing their ideas and finding new answers to their questions will help save lives if similar eruptions ever occur. They are always trying to figure out better ways to predict volcanic activity.

No volcanic eruption since Krakatau has been as deadly.

Krakatau has had many smaller eruptions since 1883.

A New Island

A new island volcano called Anak Krakatau grew from the Indian Ocean between 1927 and 1930. It sits between what used to be Krakatau's Perboewatan and Danan cones. Some people who live on nearby islands are worried about the possibility of a violent explosion occurring on Anak Krakatau. They are scared that what happened in 1883 could play out a second time in the Sunda Strait.

The Explosive History of an Island

416 C.E.

Many small volcanic eruptions create the island of Krakatau.

May 1883

Earthquakes and small volcanic eruptions begin on Krakatau.

Not Much to Fear Right Now

Right now, most scientists believe the volcanic activity on Anak Krakatau does not pose an immediate threat. Several geologists have said the island is not large enough or filled with enough magma to cause widespread destruction. Scientists are keeping a close eye on the situation, though. No one can afford to forget how one volcano changed the world in 1883!

August 27, 1883
Four major volcanic explosions on Krakatau kill 36,417 people.

August 26, 1883
Eruptions on Krakatau grow more explosive and dangerous.

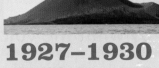

1927–1930
A new island called Anak Krakatau rises in the Sunda Strait.

For more than 100 years, people have remained interested in the story of Krakatau's eruption.

Gone but Not Forgotten

Krakatau no longer towers above ocean waves in the Sunda Strait. Yet the story of the famous volcanic island continues to be told around the world. Artists, filmmakers, writers, teachers, and scientists have kept the tale of Krakatau alive in modern times. People have remained fascinated by what the volcano was more than a century ago—an amazing, violent force of nature. ★

Number of people living on Krakatau in 1883: 0

Number of years Krakatau was quiet before 1883: more than 200

Number of major volcanic explosions on Krakatau on August 27: 4

Time of the most powerful explosion on August 27: 10:02 a.m.

Distance from Krakatau at which the 10:02 a.m. blast was heard: 3,000 mi. (5,000 km)

Maximum height of the tsunami waves on August 27: 120 ft. (37 m)

Number of towns and villages destroyed by tsunamis on August 27: 295

Number of people killed on August 27: 36,417

Amount that average world temperatures dropped after August 27: 2.2°F (1.2°C).

Did you find the truth?

F Krakatau looks almost the same as it did in 1883.

T The eruptions on Krakatau affected weather around the world.

Resources

Books

Branley, Franklyn Mansfield. *Volcanoes*. New York: Collins, 2008.

Claybourne, Anna. *The World's Most Amazing Volcanoes*. Chicago: Raintree, 2009.

Fradin, Judy, and Dennis Fradin. *Volcanoes*. Washington, DC: National Geographic, 2007.

Levy, Matthys, and Mario Salvadori. *Earthquakes, Volcanoes, and Tsunamis: Projects and Principles for Beginning Geologists*. Chicago: Chicago Review Press, 2009.

Lim, Robin. *Indonesia*. Minneapolis: Lerner Publishing Group, 2010.

Orme, David, and Helen Orme. *Tsunamis*. New York: Children's Press, 2006.

Stiefel, Chana. *Tsunamis*. New York: Children's Press, 2009.

Winchester, Simon. *The Day the World Exploded: The Earthshaking Catastrophe at Krakatoa*. New York: Collins, 2007.

Organizations and Web Sites

Discovery Channel—Krakatoa: Volcano of Destruction
http://dsc.discovery.com/convergence/krakatoa/krakatoa.html
Visit this site to explore a virtual volcano and survivors' stories.

San Diego State University Department of Geological Sciences: How Volcanoes Work
www.geology.sdsu.edu/how_volcanoes_work/Krakatau.html
Check out this site for more information what about happened on the island in 1883.

Scholastic—General Facts About Volcanoes
www2.scholastic.com/browse/article.jsp?id=4886
Read an interview with an expert geologist about volcanoes.

Places to Visit

The Museum of Science
1 Science Park
Boston, MA 02114
(617) 723-2500
www.mos.org/
exhibits_shows/live_
presentations&d=4451
Tour exhibits that show how volcanoes work and where eruptions are currently occurring across the world.

Smithsonian National Museum of Natural History
10th Street and
Constitution Avenue NW
Washington, DC 20560
(202) 633-1000
www.mnh.si.edu
See volcanic rocks and learn more about past eruptions.

Important Words

active volcanoes (AK-tiv vuhl-KAY-noz)—volcanoes that have recently erupted, are erupting, or are likely to erupt

atmosphere (AT-muhss-fihr)—the air surrounding Earth

climate (KLYE-mit)—the normal or average weather of an area

cones (KOHNZ)—mountains that form around volcanic vents

crust (KRUHST)—Earth's outer layer

eruptions (i-RUHP-shuhnz)—activities that occur when pressure forces lava, dust, ashes, gas, and pieces of rock out of a volcano's vent

geography (jee-AH-gruh-fee)—features of Earth's surface

geologists (jee-AH-luh-jests)—scientists who study the rocks and other matter that make up Earth

lava (LAH-vuh)—magma that reaches Earth's surface

magma (MAG-muh)—hot liquid rock that flows through a volcano's vent

pumice (PUH-muhss)—a type of volcanic rock

tsunamis (soo-NAH-meez)—large, powerful sea waves that are often destructive

vent (VENT)—opening in Earth's crust

Index

Page numbers in **bold** indicate illustrations

About the Author

Peter Benoit is educated as a mathematician but has many other interests. He has taught and tutored high school and college students for many years, mostly in math and science. He also runs summer workshops for writers and students of literature. Mr. Benoit has also written more than 2,000 poems. His life has been one committed to learning. He lives in Greenwich, New York.

PHOTOGRAPHS © 2011: Alamy Images: 24 (Koen Broker), 5 bottom, 18 (Classic Images), 25 (Phil Degginger), 17, 23 (Mary Evans Picture Library), 26 (Mark Eveleigh), 38 (Anna Latimer), 40 left (North Wind Picture Archives), 39 (Stocktrek Images, Inc.), 16 left (The Print Collector); AP Images: 34 (APTN), 8 (Achmad Ibrahim), 30 (Jack Smith), 4, 29 right inset (Ed Wray); Clifford Oliver Photography/www.cliffordoliverphotography.com: 48; Corbis Images: 29 center inset, 36 (Sergio Dorantes), 29 left inset (Hulton-Deutsch Collection), 14 (Charles O'Rear), 15, 40 right; Getty Images: 6, 41 left (Hulton Archive), 35, 42 (Carsten Peter/National Geographic); iStockphoto/Warren Goldswain: back cover; Marco Fulle/Stromboli Online: cover; NASA/Space Imaging: 32; Scholastic Library Publishing, Inc.: 44; ShutterStock, Inc.: 9, 11 (beboy), 22 (George Burba), 5 top, 16 right (Jose Gil), 28, 29 background, 41 right, 43 (Warren Goldswain), 20 (Mana Photo); The Design Lab: 10; The Granger Collection, New York: 3, 19; The Image Works: 33 (Mary Evans Picture Library), 27 (The Natural History Museum), 12 (ullstein bild).